DOCTRINES OF SALVATION

TOPIC 1 - Forgiveness

"To stop feeling angry or resentful towards (someone) for an offence or mistake"
Oxford English Dictionary

Key Points

- God's forgiveness is personal and mends our relationship with Him.

- God's forgiveness is judicial and removes our guilt before Him.

- God's forgiveness of sin depends on repentance and faith.

- A Christian's forgiveness should be unqualified and thus be a reflection of God's forgiveness.

1. Forgiveness is a key bible concept. Whether we measure its importance by the amount of space devoted to it in Scripture, the prominence it enjoyed in the Lord Jesus' teaching or its role in the salvation of man, it is a BIG subject. The two main areas where forgiveness operates are in man's relationship to God and in man's relationship to man. Since this series is designed to focus on the doctrines of salvation this handout will concentrate on forgiveness with God.

2. What is forgiveness? Basically it involves a person who has been wronged relinquishing any right he has to exact punishment or reparation for a wrong done. Secondly it involves abandoning feelings of anger towards the wrongdoer arising from the wrong suffered.

3. Salvation involves God forgiving us our sins. This necessarily means that our sins have offended God; otherwise there would be no need for His forgiveness. All sin offends God whether or not it involves wrong being done to another human being. Thus sin against another person is also sin against God. It follows from this that we require forgiveness from both man and God. By the same token sin may be committed against God without any other person being harmed. For example we can sin against God by thinking sinful thoughts even though they never translate into sinful actions.

4. God forgives sins in two ways. He forgives us our sins at salvation. This is a once for all act of God's will and pardons us for sins past and future as well as our inherited guilt "in Adam". When He forgives He does so judicially. 1 John 1:9 (below) indicates that we should continue to seek forgiveness from God after salvation. This forgiveness is not with a view to salvation from sin but as an expression of our remorse for the wrongs we continue to commit after salvation. These post-conversion sins can damage our relationship with God but not our standing in Christ. God offers His personal forgiveness to us after salvation and thus restores our personal fellowship with God.

5. While there are similarities between our forgiveness of one another and God's forgiveness of the Christian there are important differences as well.

Some differences
- God is always ready to forgive.[1] He knows when and how to forgive. We struggle to forgive and often do not know when or how to offer forgiveness. This is because we unlike God have a sinful nature and are subject to the limitations of humanity.
- God can never be blamed for sin and has never any responsibility for the issues that give rise to a need for forgiveness. When we forgive it is often the case that we are in some way to blame for the problem that gave rise to the wrong. We are also capable of feeling wronged when in truth no wrong has occurred at all.
- When we forgive it is not with a view to the eternal salvation of the wrongdoer. We forgive sins as an expression of God's grace in us and to maintain a damaged relationship.

---

[1] Cf. Matthew 12:32; Mark 3:28-29; Luke 12:10; 1 John 5:16.

Some similarities

- God offers forgiveness in order to restore a relationship broken by sin. So also human forgiveness is with a view to restoring inter-personal relationships.
- God's forgiveness of sins involves the abandonment of His right to punish the sinner for the wrong done. So also human forgiveness often involves the abandonment of any right to exact punishment or retribution against the wrongdoer.

6. Forgiveness is closely connected with although not identical to reconciliation. Both involve the restoration of relationships. Although reconciliation entails man setting aside his (unjustified) hostility to God and God setting aside His (justified) anger against us, forgiveness in salvation is a one-way process. He forgives us but He has no need to seek forgiveness from us.

7. God's ability to forgive rests on Calvary. This is because the ability to forgive, as noted above, rests on the wrong being dealt with on a proper basis and not just ignored or overlooked. When the Lord Jesus was punished on account of sin He was making forgiveness possible since the great obstacle to forgiveness, divine justice, was satisfied by the death of Christ. A human's right to demand repentance as a pre-condition of forgiveness is a right that can only be exercised in very limited circumstances and never justifies feelings of bitterness or hate.

8. God's forgiveness in salvation is unqualified and perpetual. The finality of God's forgiveness is part of the doctrine of the eternal security of the believer. Hence subsequent wrongdoing by the person forgiven does not provoke God to withdraw His forgiveness. This is because what He forgave was all our sins past, present and future – nothing we do subsequent to salvation falls outside the scope of His forgiveness. By contrast our daily enjoyment of God's forgiveness is contingent on our spiritual condition and our willingness to confess our sins.

 KEY SCRIPTURES

> [1] Blessed *is he whose* transgression *is* forgiven, *whose* sin is covered.
>
> **Psalm 32:1**

 **KEY SCRIPTURES**

20 And when he saw their faith, he said unto him, Man, thy sins are forgiven thee. 21 And the scribes and the Pharisees began to reason, saying, Who is this which speaketh blasphemies? Who can forgive sins, but God alone? 22 But when Jesus perceived their thoughts, he answering said unto them, What reason ye in your hearts? 23 Whether is easier, to say, Thy sins be forgiven thee; or to say, Rise up and walk? 24 But that ye may know that the Son of man hath power upon earth to forgive sins (he said unto the sick of the palsy), I say unto thee, Arise, and take up thy couch, and go into thine house.

Luke 5:20-24

14 In whom we have redemption through his blood, *even* the forgiveness of sins.

Colossians 1:14

9 If we confess our sins, he is faithful and just to forgive us *our* sins, and to cleanse us from all unrighteousness.

1 John 1:9

21 Then came Peter to him, and said, Lord, how oft shall my brother sin against me, and I forgive him? till seven times? 22 Jesus saith unto him, I say not unto thee, Until seven times: but, Until seventy times seven.

Matt. 18:21-22

32 And be ye kind one to another, tenderhearted, forgiving one another, even as God for Christ's sake hath forgiven you.

Ephesians 4:32

KEY QUOTES

Forgiveness on the part of one person toward another is the simplest of duties, whereas forgiveness on the part of God toward man (is) the most .... costly of undertakings. As seen in the Bible, there is an analogy between forgiveness and debt and, in the forgiveness that God exercises, the debt must be paid - though it is paid by Himself - before forgiveness can be extended.

Lewis Sperry Chafer[2]

Forgiveness does not mean that the victim will forget the offense. Forgiveness means no longer continuing to dwell on the sin that was forgiven. Forgiveness is the promise not to raise the issue again to the offender, to others or to himself. Brooding is a violation of the promise made in granting forgiveness.

Jay E. Adams[3]

---

[2] Systematic Theology 7:162–1
[3] The Christian Counselor's Manual p.65.

KEY QUESTIONS

1. What wrong has the sinner done to God that obliges him to seek God's forgiveness?

2. Is God obliged to forgive us our sins?

3. If God only forgives us when we repent, are we only obliged to forgive people that wrong us if they repent?

4. What are the differences between God's forgiveness of us and our forgiveness of one another?

TOPIC 2 –
Reconciliation

"To change from enmity to friendship"
Vine's Expository Dictionary of N.T. Words

Key Points

- Man needs to be reconciled to God.

- God took the initiative and in the death of Christ made reconciliation possible.

- To be reconciled man must respond to God's overtures.

- One day all that is opposed to God will be reconciled to Him

1. The Bible teaches that man and God are estranged from one another (e.g. Isaiah 59:2). The estrangement began in the Garden of Eden when Adam and Eve sinned. Once they had sinned God could no longer remain on friendly terms with them. He drove them out from the Garden and withdrew His fellowship. (Although the Bible is silent on the subject it seems likely that Adam and Eve were what we would call "believers" despite their responsibility for the entrance of sin. Their two children Cain and Abel certainly appreciated that sacrifice was necessary to approach God (Gen. 4:3-4) and it is likely that their parents had taught them this). We therefore learn that the consequences of the Fall for man's relationship with God were two fold. Man hid from God (Gen. 3:8) and God expelled man from His presence (Gen. 3:24). The break down in relations was mutual.

2. Despite this God took the initiative. He did not wish to be separated from his creatures. In order to achieve reconciliation He provided a basis for harmony to be restored. Reconciliation is possible because God has provided in the death of Christ the means by which man may be restored to fellowship with God. He has moved out towards us.

3. On the other hand man must accept the overtures God has made. He must accept that he is a sinner and repent of his sins. He must accept the provision made for his sins in the death of Christ. Reconciliation is therefore possible if we accept we are sinners and seek God's forgiveness. Reconciliation from the human point of view is the word that describes the restoration of his relationship with God.

4. Although the focus of the N.T. passages is on man's reconciliation to God, there is also a sense in which it is true that God is reconciled to man. The Bible presents to us a God who loves us but at the same time hates sin.[4] While we were in our sins He could have no fellowship with us.[5] Because of the change wrought in the believer by salvation he ceases to be unacceptable to God and peace can be restored. This recognition that reconciliation is mutual in no way implies that God was to blame for the estrangement or that He needed our forgiveness. It was man that defied God. God had done no wrong. Not everyone accepts that there is mutuality in biblical reconciliation. In the quotes below the two points of view are set out.

5. Reconciliation also describes the ultimate subjugation of creation to God. Colossians 1:20 and 21 contrasts the future reconciliation of "all things" with the present reconciliation of believers to God. Paul does not seem to be thinking of the material universe in his reference to "all things" since he sets them in contrast to their location ("earth" or "heaven"). This may indicate that reconciliation has to do with beings capable of choice. One day everything whether willingly or not will be reconciled to Him. In this sense reconciliation refers to the pacification of all things to Him.

---

[4] For the wrath of God is revealed from heaven against all ungodliness and unrighteousness of men, who hold the truth in unrighteousness; Rom 1:18.
[5] The foolish shall not stand in thy sight: thou hatest all workers of iniquity. Psalm 5:5.

KEY SCRIPTURES

18 And all things *are* of God, who hath reconciled us to himself by Jesus Christ, and hath given to us the ministry of reconciliation; 19 To wit, that God was in Christ, reconciling the world unto himself, not imputing their trespasses unto them; and hath committed unto us the word of reconciliation. 20 Now then we are ambassadors for Christ, as though God did beseech *you* by us: we pray *you* in Christ's stead, be ye reconciled to God. 21 For he hath made him *to be* sin for us, who knew no sin; that we might be made the righteousness of God in him.

2 Cor. 5:18-21

10 For if, when we were enemies, we were reconciled to God by the death of his Son, much more, being reconciled, we shall be saved by his life. 11 And not only *that*, but we also rejoice in God through our Lord Jesus Christ, through whom we have now received the reconciliation.[6]

Rom. 5:10

16 And that he might reconcile both unto God in one body by the cross, having slain the enmity thereby: 17 And came and preached peace to you which were afar off, and to them that were nigh.

Eph. 2:16-17

20 And, having made peace through the blood of his cross, by him to reconcile all things unto himself; by him, I *say*, whether *they be* things in earth, or things in heaven. 21 And you, that were sometime alienated and enemies in *your* mind by wicked works, yet now hath he reconciled.

Col. 1:20-21

---

6 The AV reads "atonement" but reconciliation is the correct translation.

KEY QUOTES

It is man who has given the offence to God, Col. 1. 21, yet it is God who, though offended, takes the initiative by providing a means of reconciliation through the death of Christ, Rom. 5. 10. In his clarification of justification by faith, Paul states that reconciliation is one of the many benefits that we receive through our Lord Jesus Christ, Rom. 5:11.

Brian Clatworthy[7]

Both the verb katallassō (reconciled) and the noun katallagē (reconciliation) appear in the New Testament only in Paul's writings. The terms always portray God as the reconciler and sinners as the ones reconciled, since it was human sin that ruptured the relationship between God and man (cf. Isa. 59:2). ... Thus, reconciliation is not something man does but what he receives.... Reconciliation does not happen when man decides to stop rejecting God but when God decides to stop rejecting man. It is a divine provision by which God's holy displeasure against alienated sinners is appeased, His hostility against them removed, and a harmonious relationship between Him and them established.[8]

John MacArthur

It is interesting to notice that no NT passage speaks of Christ as reconciling God to man. Always the stress is on man being reconciled. This in the nature of the case is very important. It is man's sin which has caused the enmity. It is man's sin that has had to be dealt with. Man may very well be called on in the words of 2 Cor. 5:20 to be 'reconciled to God'. Some students go on from this to suggest that Christ's reconciling activities are concerned only with man. But it is difficult to harmonize this with the general NT position. That which set up the barrier was the demand of God's holiness for uprightness in man...The barrier arises because God demands holiness in man. Therefore when the process of reconciliation has been effected it

---

[7] Precious Seed November 2012.
[8] New Testament Commentary 2 Corinthians p. 200.

KEY QUOTES

is impossible to say it is completely man-ward, and not God-ward in any sense. There must be a change from God's side if all that is involved in such expressions as 'the wrath of God' is no longer exercised towards man.[9]

Leon Morris

It is often noted that the N.T. never speaks of man reconciling God; indeed it never speaks of God being reconciled at all. He is always the reconciler, never the reconciled (e.g. 2 Cor. 5:20)... This has led many scholars to take it as axiomatic that all the enmity and all the misunderstanding are on the side of the human race... It is of course true that there is enmity on the human side (Rom. 8:7; Eph. 2:2).... Yet the N.T. makes it plain that there are barriers on God's side too. He cannot condone sin. He hates it, condemns it and opposes it.... All this is highlighted in the Genesis account of the fall of mankind.... This would be the mission of Christ. He would approach the Holy in the name of mankind, the sword would flash, the curse would be endured, and a new way would be opened up to Paradise... through the blood of Jesus (Heb. 10:19).[10]

Donald MacLeod

It is often affirmed that God never did need to be reconciled to the sinner – only the sinner to God. This is entirely erroneous and fails to take into account God's holy claims... as the late Dr Handley Moule writes "That word (katallage = reconciliation) habitually points to the pardon of an offended king than the consent of the rebel to yield to his kindness.... This is borne out by reference to non-theological passages such as Matt 5:24 where the difficulty is not so much of the would be worshipper but on the side of the injured absent brother, who needs to be propitiated' see also 1 Sam 29:4.[11]

William Hoste

---

[9] New Bible Dictionary (3rd ed.) p. 1002.
[10] Christ Crucified: understanding the Atonement p. 151.
[11] Bible Problems and Answers pp. 349-350.

KEY QUESTIONS

1. In what way does reconciliation differ from forgiveness?

2. Who was responsible for the breakdown in relations between God and man?

3. Who is it that took the initiative in seeking reconciliation?

4. Is reconciliation dependent on feeling at peace with God?

TOPIC 3 - Propitiation

"The removal of wrath by the offering of a gift"
International Standard Bible Encyclopaedia

Key Points

- Propitiation entails the removal of God's anger against sin.

- Propitiation is accomplished by the death of Christ.

- Propitiation is achieved because the death of Christ for sin is a sacrifice acceptable to God and which assuages his anger with the sinner.

1. Propitiation describes what happens when God's wrath is pacified. Since the Bible teaches that sin excites God's wrath, the question is whether there is anything that can be done to assuage that wrath. The answer is that in the death of Christ a sacrifice was offered which propitiated God. In other words the death of Christ for sin is so pleasing to God that propitiation is made. Propitiation stresses that the gift or sacrifice offered turns away His anger. A secondary but distinct idea is that the anger is exhausted in the gift or sacrifice. This concept is connected to the thought of substitution where the wrath that was rightfully ours is borne by Christ.

2. Propitiation reminds us that although it is true that God loves the world, He also hates sin and those that commit sin are the objects of His anger. He simultaneously loves His creatures and yet hates their sins and wrongdoing! The purpose of a propitiatory sacrifice is to enable God to deal with sins but forgive the sinner. Propitiation focuses on one of the great effects the sacrifice of Christ had in relation to God. It removes the cause of anger.

3. In the O.T. the words "atone" (kapar) and "atonement" (koper) are used to describe the effect of sacrifice for sin. A traditional understanding of atonement was a sacrifice that "covered" sin. Thus understood it did not remove sin but simply put it out of God's sight.[12] It was concluded therefore that atonement was to be contrasted with the "putting away" of sin by the death of Christ (Heb. 9:26). But the better view is that the doctrine of atonement of the O.T. is defective for the same reason that all O.T. sacrifices were defective namely that they had no intrinsic merit and required repetition. They were provisional and anticipative of the final sacrifice of Christ. If, as I believe, the word *kapar* means to purge or reconcile or, occasionally, to appease by means of a gift it is a doctrine that is fully recognised in the N.T. and is in no way a deficient O.T. concept.[13] Thus although atonement is not mentioned as a distinct topic in this booklet it finds its place alongside the doctrine of propitiation. It might also have been mentioned in connection with reconciliation or the doctrine of washing or cleansing.

---

[12] Vine's Complete Expository Dictionary of Old and New Testament Words p. 10.
[13] Theological Wordbook of the Old Testament. 1:453. See quote at end of chapter.

 **KEY SCRIPTURES**

...Christ Jesus: [25] Whom God hath set forth *to be* a propitiation through faith in his blood.

Rom. 3:24-25

[17] Therefore, in all things He had to be made like *His* brethren, that He might be a merciful and faithful High Priest in things *pertaining* to God, to make propitiation for the sins of the people.

Heb. 2:17

[1] My little children, these things write I unto you, that ye sin not. And if any man sin, we have an advocate with the Father, Jesus Christ the righteous: [2] And he is the propitiation for our sins: and not for ours only, but also for *the sins* of the whole world.

1 John 2:1-2

[10] Herein is love, not that we loved God, but that he loved us, and sent his Son *to be* the propitiation for our sins.

1 John 4:10

[36] He that believeth on the Son hath everlasting life: and he that believeth not the Son shall not see life; but the wrath of God abideth on him.

John 3:36

[6] Let no man deceive you with vain words: for because of these things cometh the wrath of God upon the children of disobedience.

Eph. 5:6

💬 KEY QUOTES

.....no man will ever cease to tremble, until he hold that God is propitiated solely by that expiation in which Christ endured his anger. In short, peace must be sought nowhere but in the agonies of Christ our Redeemer.[14]

John Calvin

The death of Christ propitiated God, averting His wrath and enabling Him to receive into His family those who place their faith in the one who satisfied Him. The extent of the propitiatory work of Christ is to the whole world (1 Jn 2:2), and the basis of propitiation is His shed blood (Ro 3:25).[15]

Charles Caldwell Ryrie

Whenever God's children sin, they provoke His anger. Of course, His anger is not an irrational lack of self-control, as it so often is with humans. His anger is the settled opposition of His holy nature to everything that is evil. Such opposition to sin cannot be dismissed with a wave of the hand. It requires something much more substantial, and the Bible states that it was only the cross that did this..... When the New Testament speaks of "propitiation," it means that Jesus' death on the cross for the sins of mankind appeased God's wrath against His people once and for all. ....Just as in the Old Testament God met with His people when the blood of the sin offering was sprinkled on the altar, so Christ's death brings us into fellowship with God.[16]

Holman Treasury of Key Bible Words

Kāpar - make an atonement, make reconciliation, purge.

The root *kāpar* is used some 150 times. It has been much discussed. There is an equivalent Arabic root meaning "cover," or "conceal." On the strength of this connection it has been supposed that the

---

[14] Institutes of the Christian Religion.
[15] A Survey of Bible Doctrine   .
[16] p. 370.

 **KEY QUOTES**

Hebrew word means "to cover over sin" and thus pacify the deity, making an atonement. It has been suggested that the OT ritual symbolized a covering over of sin until it was dealt with in fact by the atonement of Christ. There is, however, very little evidence for this view. The connection of the Arabic word is weak and the Hebrew root is not used to mean "cover." ... From the meaning of *kōper* "ransom," the meaning of *kāpar* can be better understood. It means "to atone by offering a substitute." The great majority of the usages concern the priestly ritual of sprinkling of the sacrificial blood thus "making an atonement" for the worshipper. There are forty-nine instances of this usage in Leviticus alone and no other meaning is there witnessed. The verb is always used in connection with the removal of sin or defilement, except for Gen 32:20; Prov 16:14; and Isa 28:18 where the related meaning of "appease by a gift" may be observed. It seems clear that this word aptly illustrates the theology of reconciliation in the OT. The life of the sacrificial animal specifically symbolized by its blood was required in exchange for the life of the worshipper.[17]

Laird Harris

---

[17] *Theological Wordbook of the Old Testament* pp. 452-453.

KEY QUESTIONS

1. How can God love us if He hates sin and those who commit sin?

2. Why does the death of Christ remove God's anger?

3. Whose sins were propitiated by the death of Christ?

4. If the death of Christ has propitiated God, why does He still punish sinners in hell?

TOPIC 4 – Redemption

Redemption - a releasing, on payment of a ransom.
Vine's Expository Dictionary of New Testament Words

Key Points

- Redemption involves God recovering ownership of something He once owned.

- God's original ownership of man was based on His creation of man.

- Redemption was accomplished by the death of Christ.

- Redemption provides God with complete ownership of the Christian, body, soul and spirit.

1. The main idea behind redemption in the N.T. is that God has purchased the believer and released him from the control of sin. Although we may sometimes speak of people "redeeming themselves", the Bible does not refer to self-redemption but to God redeeming us (Psalm 49:8). This redemption is based on the payment made for sins by the death of Christ.

2. The Greek words that are translated as "redeem" or "redemption" are sometimes simply translated 'purchase' or "bought" (see e.g. 1 Cor. 7:23) since the basic meaning of the words is the payment of a price. Redemption however is a particular type of purchase. Redemption is a payment that releases. Thus slaves were redeemed by the payment of a price. So also in salvation the Christian has been liberated by payment of a price.

3. One consequence of this is that God has acquired ownership of the Christian. He owns us body, soul and spirit. When resurrection occurs He will take ownership of our bodies by releasing them from death, the ultimate proof of the dominion of sin (Rom. 8:23). One day God through redemption will resume complete control and ownership of the world and the universe.

4. Although redemption of the soul is personal, redemption does not always involve individuals. God "redeemed" a whole nation from Egypt (Ex. 6:6; 2 Sam. 7:23). Their redemption was from human bondage through payment of the blood of the Passover lamb. In the OT animals (Lev. 27:27) could be redeemed as well as land (Jer. 32:7, 8) and slaves (Lev. 25:47-49).

 ## KEY SCRIPTURES

[8] Even as the Son of man came not to be ministered unto, but to minister, and to give his life a ransom for many.

Mt. 20:28

[7] In whom we have redemption through his blood, the forgiveness of sins, according to the riches of his grace;

Eph. 1:7

[24] Being justified freely by his grace through the redemption that is in Christ Jesus:

Rom. 3:24

[23] Ye are bought with a price; be not ye the servants of men.

1 Cor. 7:23

[23] And not only *they*, but ourselves also, which have the firstfruits of the Spirit, even we ourselves groan within ourselves, waiting for the adoption, *to wit*, the redemption of our body.

Rom. 8:23

[3] Christ hath redeemed us from the curse of the law

Gal. 3:13

KEY SCRIPTURES

[14] (The Lord Jesus).... gave himself for us to redeem us from all lawlessness and to purify for himself a people for his own possession who are zealous for good works.

Titus 2:14

[18] Forasmuch as ye know that ye were not redeemed with corruptible things, *as* silver and gold, from your vain conversation *received* by tradition from your fathers; [19] But with the precious blood of Christ, as of a lamb without blemish and without spot:

1 Pet. 1:18-19

[9] And they sung a new song, saying, Thou art worthy to take the book, and to open the seals thereof: for thou wast slain, and hast redeemed us to God by thy blood out of every kindred, and tongue, and people, and nation.

Rev. 5:9

KEY QUOTES

There was a young boy who decided to build a model yacht. He worked for weeks, making sure each detail was just right. Finally the big day arrived. He went down to the jetty and proudly put his boat into the water. As he triumphantly watched his little boat, he noticed that the wind had suddenly changed, and it was being swept out of sight. The little boy was heartbroken. Every day for a month he went back to see if his boat had been washed up on shore.

Finally, one day in the market he saw his boat in a store window. He excitedly ran into the store and told the proprietress that it was his boat. The woman only responded by saying that the boat would cost him two dollars. After pleading with her to no avail, the boy finally pulled out the money and gave it to the storeowner. As the boy was leaving the store, he said, "Little boat, you are twice mine. You are mine because I made you, and now you are mine because I bought you."

Encyclopaedia of Bible Illustrations

The doctrine of redemption declares that Christ bought us and paid the price for our deliverance from sin. The concept of redemption comes from the Greek word *agorazo* which means to go into the marketplace to buy. Six times in the Bible Christians are said to be "bought," or "redeemed," in regard to the death of Christ (1 Cor. 6:20; 7:23; 2 Peter 2:1; Rev. 5:9; 14:3-4). In 1 Corinthians 6:19-20 it states, "You are not your own; you were bought at a price. Therefore honor God with your body." The idea of a slave being bought is mentioned in 1 Corinthians 7:23, "You were bought at a price; do not become slaves of men." .....Another Greek verb used to express the intensive character of the redemption in Christ is the Greek word *exagorazo*. This is found four times in the New Testament (Gal. 3:13; 4:5; Eph. 5:16; Col. 4:5). In Galatians 3:13 we are said to be redeemed and delivered from the law which condemned us. The same thought is given in Galatians 4:5. The point is that we were not

KEY QUOTES

only "bought" by the redemption in Christ but we were taken out of the marketplace, that is, we were bought out of the market, and given security and set free as those who were formerly slaves.

Walvoord, J. F.[18]

---

[18] What We Believe p. 74.

KEY QUESTIONS

1. Why is redemption necessary?

2. Is there a difference between purchase and redemption?

3. What does Scripture mean by "the redemption of the body"?

4. If redemption involves payment of a price, what is the price and is it correct to think of it as paid to anyone?

TOPIC 5 – Sanctification

"To set apart a person or thing for the use intended by its designer"
Evangelical Dictionary of Biblical Theology

Key Points

- In salvation we are set apart to God and become saints.
- The lives of Christians should be set apart to God and should be marked by practical holiness.
- Sanctification involves separation from unwholesome or unscriptural influences.
- One day the saints will be taken out of the world but meanwhile we are called to live holy lives in the world.

1. "Sanctification" means the dedication or setting aside of someone or something to God. The Greek word for "sanctification" *(hagiasmos)* is also translated in some places "holiness". Holiness and sanctification are one and the same. Although it is commonly thought that sanctification is all about becoming more spiritual and less sinful, the word often does not have that connotation. The Lord Jesus for example said "I sanctify myself" (John 17:19) and He could not become more holy. What He meant was that He sanctified or dedicated Himself to the work of Calvary; cf. John 10. 36. God is throughout scripture described as "holy". This does not mean that He had to be set apart but that He was always set apart from the creation and its sin.

2. In the O.T. the first thing that God sanctified was a day. The Sabbath was set apart from other days for God (Gen. 2:3). In the O.T. sanctification is often accompanied by the performance of certain rituals. People were sanctified by ritual washing (Exod. 19:10, 14), altars were sanctified by the sprinkling of

blood (Exod. 29:37) and vessels were sanctified by the application of oil (Exod. 40:11).

3. In the N.T. the use of ritual as a means of sanctification disappears. Sanctification becomes a spiritual reality based on the death of Christ. A common name for describing Christians in the N.T. is "saint". This means a sanctified one. The word "saint" describes every Christian and is not a status which is gradually attained (Acts 20. 32; Eph. 5:26; Heb. 10. 10). Thus believers whose lives were very dubious were described as "saints" (1 Cor. 1:2, 30; 6:11).

4. In the N.T. Scriptures we discover a great variety of things may be sanctified e.g. food (1Tim 4:5) and marriage (1 Cor. 7:14). If I eat food to give me the energy to live for God that food is sanctified. If a marriage is entered into with a mutual desire to please God, that marriage is too sanctified. There are "holy" women (1 Peter 3:5) and "holy" men (2 Peter 1:21), "holy" prophets (2 Peter 3:2) and "holy" apostles (Eph 3:5). Anything or anyone that is dedicated to God is "holy".

5. While sanctification and justification occur simultaneously at salvation they refer to different aspects of salvation. Justification involves God removing our guilt whereas sanctification involves His dedication of the believer to service.

6. God desires that what Christians are positionally they should be practically (Romans 6:19; 12:1; 1 Thess. 4. 3; 1 Pet 1:15, 16). Thus Christians should not be involved in activities that are sinful or which detract from their service to God.

7. Three agents of sanctification are emphasised in Scripture: (a) the Holy Spirit (1 Cor. 6:11; 2 Thess. 2:13; 1 Pet. 1:2), (b) the Son (Heb. 10:10), and (c) the Truth of God (John 17:17; Eph. 5:26).

8. Sanctification sometimes refers to God's activities with people while they are under conviction of sin or His ordering of their lives before their conversion so that they come to Christ (1 Pet. 1:2; 2 Thess. 2:13). This does not mean that they are saints before conversion but that God takes special dealings with them.

9. God's ultimate purpose for us is our complete dedication to Him (1 John 3:2; Rom 8:29). One day we will be absolutely sanctified to God.

 **KEY SCRIPTURES**

¹ Paul, called to be an apostle of Jesus Christ through the will of God, and Sosthenes our brother, ² Unto the church of God which is at Corinth, to them that are sanctified in Christ Jesus, called to be saints, with all that in every place call upon the name of Jesus Christ our Lord, both theirs and ours:

1 Cor. 1:1-2

⁹ ... Be not deceived: neither fornicators, nor idolaters, nor adulterers, nor effeminate, nor abusers of themselves with mankind, ¹⁰ Nor thieves, nor covetous, nor drunkards, nor revilers, nor extortioners, shall inherit the kingdom of God. ¹¹ And such were some of you: but ye are washed, but ye are sanctified, but ye are justified in the name of the Lord Jesus, and by the Spirit of our God.

1 Cor. 6:9-11

² Elect according to the foreknowledge of God the Father, through sanctification of the Spirit, unto obedience and sprinkling of the blood of Jesus Christ: Grace unto you, and peace, be multiplied.

1 Peter 1:2

¹⁰ We are sanctified through the offering of the body of Jesus Christ once for all.

Heb. 10:10

¹⁹ I speak after the manner of men because of the infirmity of your flesh: for as ye have yielded your members servants to uncleanness and to iniquity unto iniquity; even so now yield your members servants to righteousness unto holiness.

Rom. 6:19

³ For this is the will of God, even your sanctification, that ye should abstain from fornication:

1 Thess. 4:3

 **KEY QUOTES**

There is a sanctification that is absolute and complete and is true of every individual who has put their trust unreservedly in Christ Jesus for Salvation. This sanctification is not progressive and is equally as true of the believer as his Justification (1 Cor. 6.11), it is therefore unrelated to any moral or practical change in the life. The believer is sanctified by faith in Christ Jesus (Acts 26.18)....

There is also in God's Word what might be termed relative sanctification... The ground around the bush that burned with fire was said by God to be "holy ground" (Exodus 3. 1-6). The Mountain of Transfiguration is called by the Apostle Peter "the Holy Mount" (2 Pet. 1.18)... Our food is sanctified by the word of God and prayer (I Tim. 4.4-5). ... All of this relates to sanctification by association. The ground in Exodus 3 did not change materially nor did the Mount of Transfiguration—they were "Holy" because the Lord was there. ... food is sanctified by God's word and His people's prayers... the food (does not) undergo any material change. ... An appreciation of this teaching helps in an understanding of Hebrews 10.29 where the apostate is under consideration....

There is also in God's word what might be termed ecclesiastical sanctification (2 Tim. 2.21). Few things can be more displeasing to God than the propagation of error under the name of Christ. Where this is irreversibly accepted, the plain duty of the child of God who desires to be a vessel unto honour, sanctified and meet for the Master's use is to purge himself out from or away from those vessels to dishonour. The honour of the Lord and one's usefulness to Him demands this at all times and more especially in a day when unity at all costs is the cry of Christendom.

There is also throughout the word of God a clear call to practical sanctification. The experience of the New Birth and the possession of a New Nature must create within the child of God a deep desire for Pure, Holy, Sanctified living. The Apostle

KEY QUOTES

Peter has this to say "But as he which hath called you is holy, so be ye holy in all manner of conversation" (1 Pet. 1.15).

Albert Leckie[19]

The word sanctify means to set apart (it has the same root as the words *saint* and *holy*). For the Christian, sanctification has three aspects. First, the believer has been set apart by his position in the family of God. This is usually called positional sanctification.... It is true of every believer regardless of his spiritual condition.... there is also the experiential aspect of sanctification. Because we have been set apart we are to be increasingly set apart in our daily lives (1 Pet. 1:16). In the positional sense no one is more sanctified than another, but in the experiential aspect it is quite correct to speak of one believer as being more sanctified than another. All the exhortations of the New Testament concerning spiritual growth are pertinent to this progressive and experiential facet of sanctification. There is also a sense in which we will not be fully set apart to God until our position and practice are brought into perfect accord, and this will occur only when we see Christ and become as He is (1 John 3:1–3). Thus there is an aspect to sanctification which is often called ultimate or future sanctification and which awaits our complete glorification with resurrection bodies (Eph 5:26–27; Jude 24–25).

Charles Caldwell Ryrie[20]

---

[19] Assembly Testimony Sept./Oct 1984.
[20] A Survey of Bible Doctrine.

KEY QUESTIONS

1. When does a Christian become a saint?

2. Why does God want us to be holy?

3. Is it possible to live a separated life without leaving the world completely?

4. Is separation just concerned with moral wrongdoing?

TOPIC 6 –
Justification

"The event whereby persons are set or declared to be in right relation to God"
The Anchor Yale Bible Dictionary

Key Points
- Justification in the Bible depends exclusively on the death of Christ.
- Justification is a final verdict pronounced by God.
- Justification is received by faith.
- Justification is inspired by God's grace.

1. In November, 1515, Martin Luther, professor of sacred theology at the University of Wittenberg, began to study the Epistle to the Romans in order to expound it to his students. The experience was to change his life. He later wrote -

I grasped the truth that <u>the righteousness of God is that righteousness whereby, through grace and sheer mercy, He justifies us by faith</u>. Thereupon I felt myself to be reborn and to have gone through open doors into paradise. The whole of Scripture took on a new meaning, and whereas before "the righteousness of God" had filled me with hate, now it became unto me inexpressively sweet in greater love. This passage of Paul became to me a gateway to heaven.

The Reformation can be dated to the moment he nailed his ninety-five theses on the door of the Castle Church of Wittenberg on 31 October 1517. He was outraged at the sale of "indulgences" by the Roman Catholic Church, which promised remission of sins in return for the payment of money. The 95 theses were Luther's attempt to expose the doctrinal and moral corruption of the Roman Catholic Church. Thesis 86 asks for example "Why does the pope, whose wealth today is greater than the wealth of the richest Crassus, build the basilica of Saint Peter with the money of poor believers rather than with his own money?" The debate he sparked spread through Europe. The Roman Catholic Church lost many adherents and new churches sprang up. Although the Roman Catholic Church no longer sells "indulgences" and has corrected some of the more extreme examples of its corruption, it still teaches that acceptance by God does not depend exclusively on faith. It teaches that justification depends on the sacrament of baptism, is maintained by penance and can be lost by "mortal" sin.

2. The word "justify" *(dikeoo)* means to clear from guilt and to declare righteous. Those God has justified are as a result "just" in the eyes of God.

3. Justification is a key N.T. truth since it deals with the most fundamental question of all – how can we be right before God? The Lord Jesus and the apostles taught no man has ever lived a perfectly upright life except for the Lord Jesus Himself. He is the "Just" (Acts 3:14) whereas we are the "unjust" (1 Peter 3:18). Because of our sinful nature we will never be right in the eyes of God. But God is willing to justify us. He does so if we repent from our sins and place our trust in Him. Hence what is crucial is our attitude or disposition to God. This requires a change on our part because our natural inclination is to oppose God.

4. When He justifies man God is acting as a judge and is clearing the sinner of his guilt. That happens at the moment of conversion but will be fully revealed when we reach heaven.

5. Justification does not involve the removal of the capacity for sin. It is instead a verdict. God clears the sinner of his guilt because his penalty has been borne by Christ and gets the benefit of that when he trusts Christ for salvation. God will not hold the sinner answerable for his sins but will regard him as one who has no sins to answer for. He is redefined as one who is "in Christ" and no longer "in Adam".

6. A man or woman is justified at the moment of their salvation. When faith is placed in God He justifies the believer. The means of justification on our part is faith.

7. God's grace and love are the inspiration for salvation. He justifies because He desires to save man. No matter how gracious God was however He would not do anything that was wrong. Simply "letting us off" was not possible. Sin is a crime and a breach of God's law which must be punished. The cross is God's solution to the problem of our guilt. In punishing His Son for our sin He is relieved of the necessity of punishing us. Having punished Christ He need not punish us too. Of course the benefit of the cross is only experienced by those who accept it. Salvation is a gift God offers. If salvation is rejected God will punish those that have rejected His offer. The fact that the Lord Jesus bore the punishment for sin in all its forms does not mean that God cannot punish a man for his own sins. On believing God the believer is given eternal life, his sins are forgiven, he receives the Holy Spirit – but central to all his blessings is the truth that God now holds him to be justified and acquitted from all guilt.

8. The ability to live righteously is quite different. The fact that God has justified us is a positional truth and has no direct bearing on our personal righteousness. However at salvation God also gives the believer a new nature through new birth, the indwelling Spirit, and written guidance in the form of Scripture to assist him in his development of personal righteousness.

9. It is perhaps the central truth of the N.T. Our salvation depends on it. The cross is the foundation for it. Although it is a dangerous thing to rank doctrines in order of importance it may be observed that in Paul's greatest discussion of salvation, the Roman epistle, justification is its central point. It is because God can clear the guilt of the sinner that He can impart new life and forgive the sinner.

10. As we have noticed above justification and righteousness are interconnected. A just man is a righteous man. The Bible does call some people "just" (Simeon - Luke 2:25) and "righteous" (Abel - Matthew 23:35) not because they never sinned or were justified by faith (though they were) but because their lives were righteous and just. But no man, save the Lord Jesus, is absolutely just or righteous.

KEY SCRIPTURES

[13] The publican, standing afar off, would not lift up so much as *his* eyes unto heaven, but smote upon his breast, saying, God be merciful to me a sinner. [14] I tell you, this man went down to his house justified *rather* than the other.

Luke 18:13-14

[33] Who shall lay anything to the charge of God's elect? *It is* God that justifieth.

Rom. 8:33

[5] For Moses describeth the righteousness which is of the law, That the man which doeth those things shall live by them.

Rom. 10:5

[20] Therefore by the deeds of the law there shall no flesh be justified in his sight: for by the law *is* the knowledge of sin.

Rom. 3:20

[16] ...a man is not justified by the works of the law, but by the faith of Jesus Christ, even we have believed in Jesus Christ, that we might be justified by the faith of Christ, and not by the works of the law: for by the works of the law shall no flesh be justified.

Gal. 2:16

[28] Therefore we conclude that a man is justified by faith without the deeds of the law.

Rom. 3:28

[39] And by him all that believe are justified from all things, from which ye could not be justified by the law of Moses.

Acts 13:39

[23] For all have sinned, and come short of the glory of God; [24] Being justified freely by his grace through the redemption that is in

KEY SCRIPTURES

Christ Jesus: ²⁵ Whom God hath set forth *to be* a propitiation through faith in his blood, to declare his righteousness for the remission of sins that are past, through the forbearance of God; ²⁶ To declare, *I say*, at this time his righteousness: that he might be just, and the justifier of him which believeth in Jesus.

Rom. 3:23-26

¹⁸ Therefore as by the offence of one *judgment came* upon all men to condemnation; even so by the righteousness of one *the free gift came* upon all men unto justification of life. ¹⁹ For as by one man's disobedience many were made sinners, so by the obedience of one shall many be made righteous.

Rom. 5:18-19

⁹ Much more then, being now justified by his blood, we shall be saved from wrath through him.

Rom. 5:9

²⁴ Jesus ... ²⁵ Who was delivered for our offences, and was raised again for our justification.

Rom. 4:24-25

³³ Who shall lay any thing to the charge of God's elect? *It is* God that justifieth. ³⁴ Who *is* he that condemneth? *It is* Christ that died, yea rather, that is risen again, who is even at the right hand of God.

Rom. 8:33-34

KEY QUOTES

Justification is not because of any overlooking, suspending, or altering of God's righteous demands, but because in Christ all of His demands have been fulfilled. Christ's perfect life of obedience to the law and His atoning death which paid its penalty are the bases for our justification (Rom. 5:9).

Charles Caldwell Ryrie[21]

In theology, justification is the judicial act of God declaring one to be righteous by imputation of righteousness to him. It is judicial not experiential, and all believers in Christ are equally justified.

John Walvoord[22]

---

[21] A Survey of Bible Doctrine.
[22] Jesus Christ Our Lord.

KEY QUESTIONS

1. If I am a sinner and deserve punishment for my sins how is it possible for God to declare me righteous?

2. If I am justified by God does that mean I stop sinning?

3. How does justification differ from forgiveness?

4. Is it possible for a Christian to do anything that would lead to him ceasing to be justified?

TOPIC 7 – Adoption

"The act of God by which believers become members of 'God's family' with all the privileges and obligations of family membership"
Baker Encyclopaedia of the Bible

Key Points
- Adoption brings us into the family of God.
- Adoption confers all the privileges of true sonship on the Christian.
- Christ was eternally the Father's Son whereas the believer becomes a son by adoption.
- New birth stresses the new life of a babe in Christ whereas adoption stresses the privileges and responsibility of an adult son.

1. The best-known example of adoption in Scripture is the "adoption" of Moses by Pharaoh's daughter (Ex. 2:10; Acts 7:21[23]). He exchanged a life of danger for one of security. He exchanged poor parents for the wealth of the royal family. He had been the son of slaves and became the son of a king. Another example is Esther who was adopted (see Esther 2:7, 15) by her uncle Mordecai. Moses' experience is a particularly vivid illustration of the adoption of the believer as taught in the N.T. In Romans and Galatians in particular Paul uses the idea of "adoption" to describe the way God changes "children of wrath" (Eph. 2:3; 6:4) into "sons of God".

2. There does not seem to have been any formal mechanism for adoption in the O.T. for Israel. When the N.T. was written adoption was possible under both Greek and Roman Law. Many of the Roman emperors were adopted. Augustus who was Emperor when the Lord Jesus was born was adopted. So were Nero, Caligula and Hadrian to name a few. In the UK today if a couple wish to adopt they must go through a lengthy and detailed legal process that often costs a lot of money. When children are adopted they are not just being "looked after" or fostered but acquire all the rights of a natural child

---

[23] And when he was exposed, Pharaoh's daughter <u>adopted him</u> and brought him up as her own son. (ESV)

of the adopting family. This is what adoption means in the N.T. Adoption describes how people who had no claim on God are brought into His family and acquire all the privileges and responsibilities of true sons.

3. Adoption is also used to contrast the relationship Christians have to God with that which Israel had under Law. Under the Old Testament Law Israel was like a servant whereas under grace the believer is like an adopted son. The law brought bondage whereas grace brings freedom.

4. Although we are described as sons of God in Scripture our sonship differs from that of the Lord Jesus. He was always the Son whereas we had to be brought into the family to achieve the status of son. He was never adopted. Even so the sonship of the believer has certain similarities with the sonship of Christ. He was intimate with the Father and likewise the believer may enjoy intimacy with God. His sonship was revealed by the fact that He was led by the Spirit and so too as we are led by the Spirit we reveal our sonship. Our sonship is a faint reflection of His full sonship.

 **KEY SCRIPTURES**

¹⁴ For as many as are led by the Spirit of God, they are the sons of God. ¹⁵ For ye have not received the spirit of bondage again to fear; but ye have received the Spirit of adoption, whereby we cry, Abba, Father. ¹⁶ The Spirit itself beareth witness with our spirit, that we are the children of God:

Romans 8:14-16

²³ ...ourselves also, which have the firstfruits of the Spirit, even we ourselves groan within ourselves, waiting for the adoption, *to wit*, the redemption of our body.

Rom. 8:23

⁴ Who are Israelites; to whom *pertaineth* the adoption, and the glory, and the covenants, and the giving of the law, and the service *of God*, and the promises; ⁵ Whose *are* the fathers, and of whom as concerning the flesh Christ *came*, who is over all, God blessed for ever. Amen

Rom. 9:4-5

⁴ God sent forth his Son, made of a woman, made under the law, ⁵ To redeem them that were under the law, that we might receive the adoption of sons. ⁶ And because ye are sons, God hath sent forth the Spirit of his Son into your hearts, crying, Abba, Father. ⁷ Wherefore thou art no more a servant, but a son; and if a son, then an heir of God through Christ.

Gal. 4:4-7

⁵ Having predestinated us unto the adoption of children by Jesus Christ to himself, according to the good pleasure of his will.

Eph. 1:5

KEY QUOTES

... adoption means.... all the privileges.. of independence from tutors and governors – and (the) liberty of a full-grown man. Hence the Christian is enjoined to "stand fast" in the freedom wherewith Christ has made him free, and not to be "entangled again with the yoke of bondage" (which is evidently an allusion to the legal or merit system, Gal 5:1), Spiritual adoption imposes also the responsibilities belonging to full matureness.[24]

Lewis Sperry Chafer

The relationship of adoption is different from that of new birth; through the latter we are born into the family, but adoption gives us position, rights and privileges in the family. We are sons and daughters, 2 Cor. 6:18, but now the daughters have all the privileges of sonship that would have been denied to them in families in New Testament times.[25]

Howard Barnes

* Bibliotheca Sacra Volume 107 1950 p. 428.
Precious Seed 1992 vol. 43.

KEY QUESTIONS

1. Why does adoption contrast the difference between Israel's relationship with Jehovah and the Christian's relationship with the Father?

2. What is the difference between new birth and adoption?

3. Why is adoption a good illustration for the Christian's relationship with God?

4. What is the meaning of the phrase "we cry Abba, Father"?

TOPIC 8 –
New Birth and Regeneration

"The impartation of spiritual life to those who are by nature dead in trespasses and sins"
Easton's Bible Dictionary

Key Points
- New birth is a spiritual work in contrast to natural birth which is a physical work.
- New birth occurs at the moment of salvation and brings a new nature into being.
- New birth is a precondition of entry into the Kingdom in both its visible or invisible forms.
- New birth by the Spirit is to be distinguished from the indwelling of the Spirit.

1. While man is made in the image of God and possesses a soul and conscience, these aspects of his nature do not enable him to live as God would wish. In order for that to happen God must change man. In salvation God imparts a new nature. The new nature is responsive to God. This does not mean that the old nature, called in the Bible "the flesh", is eradicated but it now has a rival.

2. The new nature is not visible on x-ray but ought to be visible in a change of attitude and interests. The new nature is provided at the moment of new birth. The most common way of describing the moment of regeneration is being "born again". Other similar expressions are "second" birth, "new" birth and being "born from above". New birth does not precede salvation as some suggest. Peter and James both describe new birth as coming though hearing the word of God. This indicates that new birth coincides with our acceptance of that word. Hence the new birth occurs by a work of God which coincides with our belief of the truth.

3. While believers in the O.T. were counted righteous because of their faith in God there is no clear indication that O.T. believers were regenerated by the Holy Spirit.   New birth as a distinctive doctrine makes its first appearance in the teaching of the Lord Jesus in John ch 3. While the dispensation of grace and the Church age had not yet commenced when He taught Nicodemus, it is plain that much of His teaching is anticipative. The O.T. had taught that the New Covenant would be characterised by the work of the Spirit. So while it may be correct to acknowledge that O.T. believers had divine life it may not be possible to say that a regenerating work of the Spirit had been done in them in the way taught in the N.T.

4. New birth in John ch 3 procures entrance into the kingdom. This kingdom in John's gospel is that inaugurated by Christ and presaged by John Baptist. It is presently invisible but during the Millennium will be manifested. The church is part of the kingdom but the kingdom is not co-extensive with the Church. It is clear that the Lord Jesus was teaching new truth as He explained to Nicodemus that salvation is not based on keeping the Law but on being "born again" by the Spirit. I think those that argue that Nicodemus should have appreciated that the national regeneration of Ezekiel 37:14 was the same as individual new birth are being somewhat hard on the man (and possibly inaccurate).

5. Linking the Lord's teaching on new birth with the epistles indicates that it marks the end of the "old" man. Although some passages speak of the putting on of the new man as a decisive "once for all" act which coincides with the putting off of the "old man", Scripture also indicates that the "new man" requires to be cultivated and the old man (or flesh) needs to be "starved". The old nature remains with us until the moment of our translation to heaven although judicially we are treated as new men in Christ Jesus.

6. The new birth is a divine work. No child ever chose the moment of its birth. So likewise the Spirit alone imparts life. It is clear however from John ch 3 that alongside the Lord's teaching about the new birth, the Saviour also taught that salvation is a consequence of faith in the Lord Jesus, the One who was "lifted up". Likewise the Saviour taught Nicodemus that those who are born

again and who have received eternal life are characterised by a desire to "come to the light". Their faith is known by their works.

KEY SCRIPTURES

³ Verily, verily, I say unto thee, Except a man be born again, he cannot see the kingdom of God.

John 3:3

⁵ Jesus answered, Verily, verily, I say unto thee, Except a man be born of water and of the Spirit, he cannot enter into the kingdom of God. That which is born of the flesh is flesh; and that which is born of the Spirit is spirit.

John 3:5-6

²³ Being born again, not of corruptible seed, but of incorruptible, by the word of God, which liveth and abideth for ever.

1 Peter 1:23

¹⁸ Of his own will begat he us with the word of truth, that we should be a kind of firstfruits of his creatures.

James 1:18

⁵ Not by works of righteousness which we have done, but according to his mercy he saved us, by the washing of regeneration, and renewing of the Holy Ghost;

Titus 3:5

⁹ Lie not one to another, seeing that ye have put off the old man with his deeds; ¹⁰ And have put on the new *man*, which is renewed in knowledge after the image of him that created him:

Col 3:9-10

⁶ Knowing this, that our old man is crucified with *him*, that the body of sin might be destroyed, that henceforth we should not serve sin.

Rom. 6:6

KEY SCRIPTURES

24 Put on your new nature, created to be like God—truly righteous and holy.

Eph. 4:24 N.L.T.

16 *This* I say then, Walk in the Spirit, and ye shall not fulfil the lust of the flesh. 17 For the flesh lusteth against the Spirit, and the Spirit against the flesh: and these are contrary the one to the other: so that ye cannot do the things that ye would.

Gal. 5:16-17

17 Therefore if any man *be* in Christ, *he is* a new creature: old things are passed away; behold, all things are become new.

2 Cor. 5:17

KEY QUOTES

There are three terms that, while they are closely related, must be distinguished. These are "quickening"; "born again" and... "regeneration"....The main idea in quickening is the impartation of divine life. ... Thus we read, "It is the Spirit that quickeneth ..." Jn.6.63....Many are the references which prove that the Father Himself is involved. Eph.2.1, 5; Col.2.13....(T)he expression, *"born again"* implies initiation to the family. It is when we are born naturally that we become part of our father's family. So it is spiritually. It is only when we are "born again" that we enter the family of God. This does not come about by baptism, natural family ties, religious observances or anything else done by or on a person by themselves or any other human. New birth is from God. Hence the words of the Lord Jesus to Nicodemus, "Verily, verily, I say unto thee, Except a man be born again, he cannot see the kingdom of God ... Marvel not that I said unto thee, Ye must be born again" Jn.3.3,7.... We are never said to be born of Christ. We learn from 1 Pet.1.23 that God using His word, produces it.[26]

Brian Currie

In the Reformed concept of the order of salvation, regeneration is said to precede faith. This is based on the logic that a sinner, dead in his trespasses and sins, must be given new life (i.e., regenerated) so that he or she is then able to believe (subsequently). Although this may be seen as a logical order, it is undebatably not a chronological one. Regeneration does not precede faith chronologically. In my judgment, it is unwise to state this idea even in only a logical sense, for it is well nigh impossible to eliminate chronological implications from the concept even when it is only logically presented. One might turn the logic around and argue that if a sinner has the new life and then believes, why does he or she need to believe, for that one already has been regenerated. If there is any chronological sequence

---

[26] The Glory of His Grace ch.9 Regeneration.

in regeneration followed by faith, then there must be an interval, however brief, during which the person is regenerated without having believed. Such a monstrous idea is completely unbiblical. Regeneration and faith occur simultaneously.[27]

Charles Caldwell Ryrie

The Holy Spirit pp. 90-91.

KEY QUESTIONS

1. Why must we be born again to enter the Kingdom?

2. What kind of life comes into being at new birth?

3. Which member of the Godhead brings about new birth?

4. Which Scriptures show that new birth is brought about by believing the Word of God?